Spot the Difference

Publications International, Ltd.

Photography from Dreamstime, Fotolia, Getty, Media
Bakery, Photos to Go, Shutterstock.com and Thinkstock

Brain Games is a registered trademark of
Publications International, Ltd.

Louis Weber, CEO
Publications International, Ltd.
8140 Lehigh Avenue
Morton Grove, IL 60053

Permission is never granted for commercial purposes.

ISBN: 978-1-68022-936-3

Manufactured in China.

8 7 6 5 4 3 2 1

A SINGLE SUBTLE CHANGE

Can you find it? Each puzzle has been subtly altered. Your job: spot the single difference. It may be a button missing from a shirt, a minor alteration in wallpaper, an animal facing a different direction, or even a reconfigured cloud. Do you have the eagle eyes to see the change?

A puzzle may consist of only two pictures or as many as six. Regardless of number, there's never more than a single change to be found. If you're stumped, you can always check the answer key in the back of the book.

Pagoda Puzzler

Answer on page 141.

Ornamentally Yours

Answer on page 141.

Squash, Anyone?

Answer on page 141.

Poinsettia Puzzle

Answer on page 141.

Mystery in Mystic

Answer on page 141.

Devilish Duty

Answer on page 141.

Scour the Towers

Answer on page 142.

Penguin Colony

Skulls 'n' Bones

Answer on page 142.

Wondrous Wall

Answer on page 142.

Capitol Gains

1

2

3

4

5

6

Answer on page 142.

A Real Corker

Answer on page 142.

Puzzling Pyrotechnics

Answer on page 143.

Carpenter Belt

Answer on page 143.

Take the Plunge . . .

Answer on page 143.

Fruit Salad

1

2

3

4

5

6

Answer on page 143.

A Model Arrangement

Answer on page 143.

Everything's Coming Up Roses

24

Answer on page 143.

Hanging Out

Are You Game?

Answer on page 144.

Saddle Blanket Bingo

Answer on page 144.

Barrel of Fun

Splash of Color

Answer on page 144.

A Snowy Ride

Answer on page 144.

Family Photo

Answer on page 145.

The Light Fantastic

Answer on page 145.

Get Up and Dance

Crypt Creep

Answer on page 145.

Perplexing Place Setting

1

2

3

4

Answer on page 145.

The Primrose Path

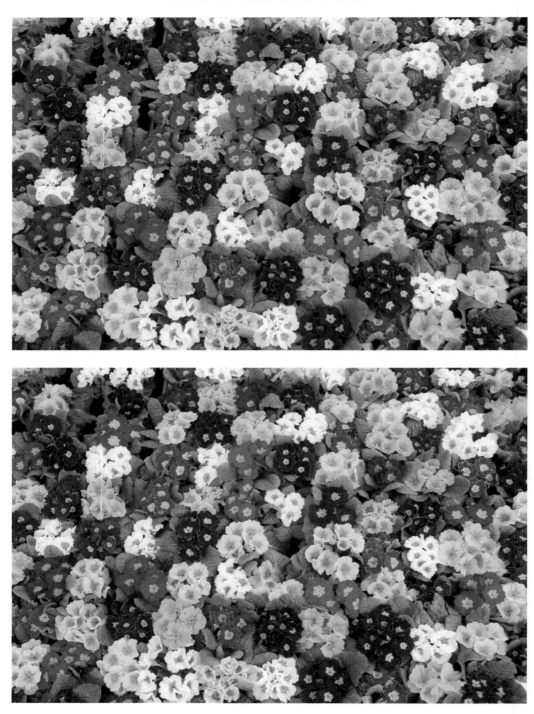

Answer on page 145.

Rest Stop

Answer on page 146.

Summertime Stroll

Answer on page 146.

Go with the Flow

Answer on page 146.

Wild Wonderland

Answer on page 146.

Bridging the Gap

Answer on page 146.

Strings Attached

Winter Wonderings

Answer on page 147.

Puzzling Paints

Have a Ball

Answer on page 147.

Polka Dot Pup

Answer on page 147.

Horse of a Different Color

Answer on page 147.

Sweetest Day

Answer on page 147.

A Tangled Web

Answer on page 148.

Vexing Vases

Answer on page 148.

Laying Low

1

2

3

4

5

6

Answer on page 148.

Bejeweled

Answer on page 148.

Do or Die

Answer on page 148.

Fascinating Fresco

Knock, Knock

Answer on page 149.

Howdy, Cowboy!

Answer on page 149.

Baffling Beads

Answer on page 149.

A Bridge Too Far

Answer on page 149.

Chest Congestion

Answer on page 149.

Spool Party

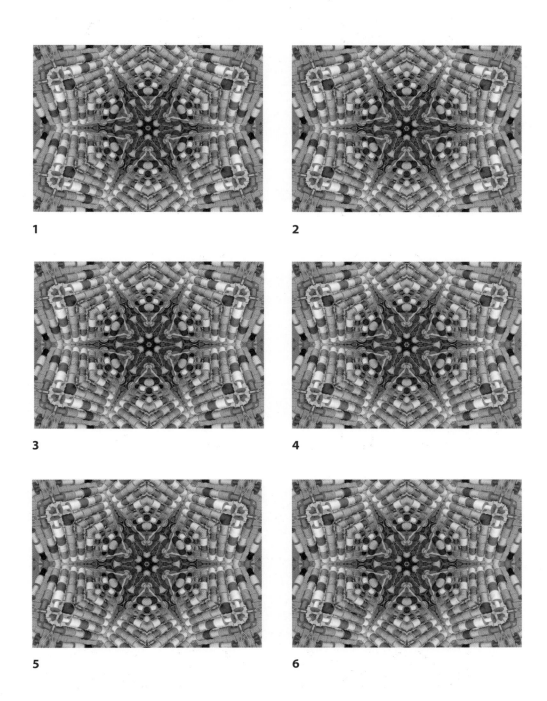

1

2

3

4

5

6

Answer on page 149.

Something's Fishy

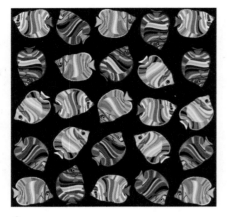

1

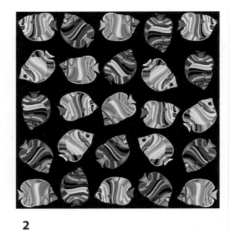

2

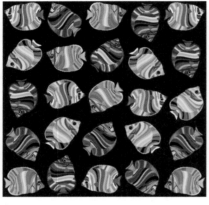

3

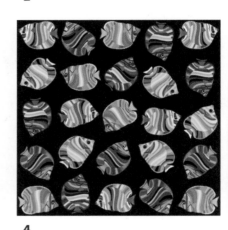

4

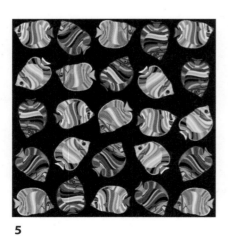

5

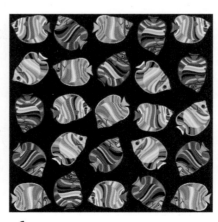

6

Answer on page 150.

Spin a Yarn

Answer on page 150.

Special Sauce

Answer on page 150.

Beautiful Boxes

Answer on page150.

All Is Calm, All Is Bright

Answer on page 150.

Piece It Together

Answer on page 150.

Seed You Later

Answer on page 151.

Nip It in the Bud

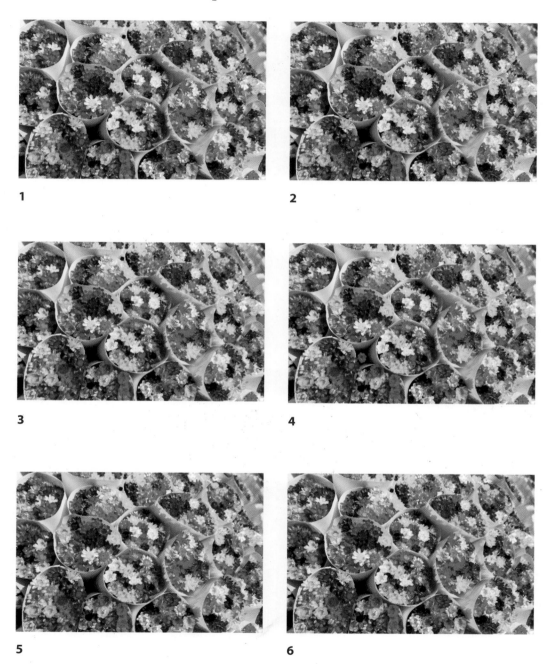

1

2

3

4

5

6

Answer on page 151.

Sink or Swim

Answer on page 151.

In a Fog

Answer on page 151.

Hoot Suite

Answer on page 151.

Carpet of Leaves

Answer on page 151.

Stick with the Classics

Answer on page 152.

Berry Good

Answer on page 152.

Out to Pasture

Answer on page 152.

Owl Be Waiting

Answer on page 152.

Cubist Theory

Answer on page 152.

Budding Romance

Answer on page 152.

Windows to the World

1

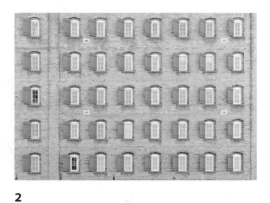

2

3

4

5

6

Answer on page 153.

Unmask the Change

Answer on page 153.

Artful Arrangement

Answer on page 153.

Whose Ear?

Answer on page 153.

Produce Results

Answer on page 153.

Petal Profusion

Answer on page 153.

Camel Creativity

Answer on page 154.

Disc-ography

Answer on page 154.

A Steady Clip

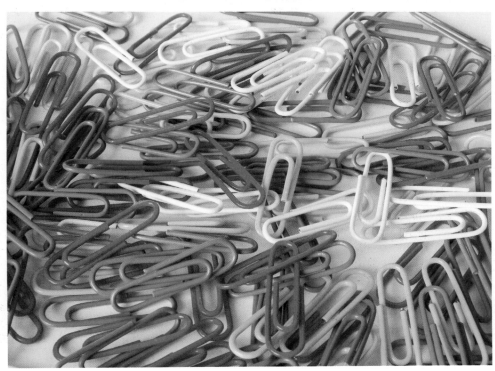

Answer on page 154.

Bing Badda Bloom

Answer on page 154.

Shard Search

Answer on page 154.

Decked-Out Dog

Answer on page 154.

A-*maize*-ing Array

Answer on page 155.

Bewildering Bikes

1

2

3

4

5

6

Answer on page 155.

Kayak Landing

Answer on page 155.

Ghosts in the Graveyard

Answer on page 155.

How Does Your Garden Grow?

Answer on page 155.

On the Lookout

Answer on page 155.

Eerie Artwork

Answer on page 156.

Ancient Architecture

Answer on page 156.

Spellbinding Stained Glass

Fall Foliage

Answer on page 156.

Take a Dip

Shopping for Treats

Answer on page 156.

Pumping Station

Answer on page 157.

Machinist's Duties

1

2

3

4

5

6

Answer on page 157.

Line Up for Lunch!

Answer on page 157.

Porch Puzzle

Answer on page 157.

Fire Truck Fun

1

2

3

4

5

6

Answer on page 157.

Sticking Together

Answer on page 157.

Pop Spot

Answer on page 158.

Industrial Indecision

1

2

3

4

5

6

Answer on page 158.

Machinery Machinations

Answer on page 158.

Shoot 'Em Up!

Answer on page 158.

Dapper Dogpatch

Answer on page 158.

Deep Sea Discovery

Answer on page 158.

Auditorium Seating

Answer on page 159.

Panel Piece

Answer on page 159.

Curve Appeal

Answer on page 159.

Tomato (Cut and) Paste

Answer on page 159.

Chilling to the Bone

Answer on page 159.

Train Travails

Answer on page 159.

Corral Challenge

Answer on page 160.

Hallway Hunt

1

2

3

4

Answer on page 160.

Answers

Pagoda Puzzler *(pages 4–5)*

Ornamentally Yours *(page 6)*

Squash, Anyone? *(page 7)*

Poinsettia Puzzle *(page 8)*

Mystery in Mystic *(page 9)*

Devilish Duty *(pages 10–11)*

■Scour the Towers *(page 12)*

■Wondrous Wall *(page 15)*

■Penguin Colony *(page 13)*

■Capitol Gains *(page 16)*
picture 3

■Skulls 'n' Bones *(page 14)*

■A Real Corker *(page 17)*

Puzzling Pyrotechnics *(pages 18–19)*

Carpenter Belt *(page 20)*

Take the Plunge . . . *(page 21)*

Fruit Salad *(page 22)*
picture 5

A Model Arrangement *(page 23)*

Everything's Coming Up Roses *(page 24)*

■Hanging Out *(page 25)*

■Barrel of Fun *(page 29)*

■Are You Game? *(pages 26–27)*

■Splash of Color *(page 30)*

■Saddle Blanket Bingo *(page 28)*

■A Snowy Ride *(page 31)*

Family Photo *(page 32)*

Crypt Creep *(page 36)*

The Light Fantastic *(page 33)*

Perplexing Place Setting *(page 37)*
picture 2

Get Up and Dance *(pages 34–35)*

The Primrose Path *(page 38)*

Rest Stop *(page 39)*

Wild Wonderland *(page 42)*

Summertime Stroll *(page 40)*

Bridging the Gap *(page 43)*

Go with the Flow *(page 41)*

Strings Attached *(pages 44–45)*

Winter Wonderings *(page 46)*

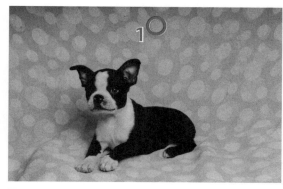

Polka Dot Pup *(page 49)*

Puzzling Paints *(page 47)*

Horse of a Different Color *(pages 50–51)*

Have a Ball *(page 48)*

Sweetest Day *(page 52)*

A Tangled Web *(page 53)*

Bejeweled *(page 57)*

Vexing Vases *(pages 54–55)*

Do or Die *(page 58)*

Laying Low *(page 56)*
picture 2

Fascinating Fresco *(page 59)*

■**Knock, Knock** *(page 60)*

■**A Bridge Too Far** *(page 63)*

■**Howdy, Cowboy!** *(page 61)*

■**Chest Congestion** *(page 64)*

■**Baffling Beads** *(page 62)*

■**Spool Party** *(page 65)*
picture 6

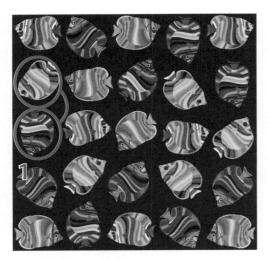

■Something's Fishy *(page 66)*
picture 1

■Spin a Yarn *(page 67)*

■Special Sauce *(page 68)*

■Beautiful Boxes *(page 69)*

■All Is Calm, All Is Bright
(page 70)

■Piece It Together *(page 71)*

Seed You Later *(page 72)*

In a Fog *(page 75)*

Nip It in the Bud *(page 73)*
picture 4

Hoot Suite *(pages 76–77)*

Sink or Swim *(page 74)*

Carpet of Leaves *(page 78)*

Stick with the Classics *(page 79)*

Owl Be Waiting *(page 82)*

Berry Good *(page 80)*

Cubist Theory *(page 83)*

Out to Pasture *(page 81)*

Budding Romance *(page 84)*

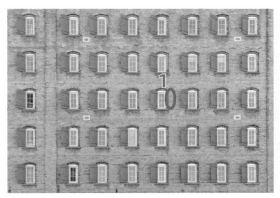

■Windows to the World *(page 85)*
picture 3

■Whose Ear? *(page 89)*

■Unmask the Change *(pages 86–87)*

■Produce Results *(page 90)*

■Artful Arrangement *(page 88)*

■Petal Profusion *(page 91)*

Camel Creativity *(pages 92–93)*

Bing Badda Bloom *(page 96)*

Disc-ography *(page 94)*

Shard Search *(page 97)*

A Steady Clip *(page 95)*

Decked-Out Dog *(pages 98–99)*

■**A-*maize*-ing Array** *(page 100)*

■**Ghosts in the Graveyard** *(page 104)*

■**Bewildering Bikes** *(page 101)*
picture 2

■**How Does Your Garden Grow?** *(page 105)*

■**Kayak Landing** *(pages 102–103)*

■**On the Lookout** *(pages 106–107)*

■Eerie Artwork *(pages 108–109)*

■Ancient Architecture *(page 110)*

■Spellbinding Stained Glass *(page 111)*

■Fall Foliage *(page 112)*

■Take a Dip *(page 113)*

■Shopping for Treats *(pages 114–115)*

■Pumping Station *(page 116)*

■Machinist's Duties *(page 117)*
picture 3

■Line Up for Lunch! *(pages 118–119)*

■Porch Puzzle *(pages 120–121)*

■Fire Truck Fun *(page 122)*
picture 2

■Sticking Together *(page 123)*

Pop Spot *(pages 124–125)*

Shoot 'Em Up! *(pages 128–129)*

Industrial Indecision *(page 126)*
picture 5

Dapper Dogpatch *(page 130)*

Machinery Machinations *(page 127)*

Deep Sea Discovery *(page 131)*

Auditorium Seating *(page 132)*

Panel Piece *(page 133)*

Curve Appeal *(page 134)*

Tomato (Cut and) Paste *(page 135)*

Chilling to the Bone *(page 136)*

Train Travails *(page 138)*

■Corral Challenge *(page 139)*

■Hallway Hunt *(page 140)*
picture 3